Simpsonville Elementary School

39508426

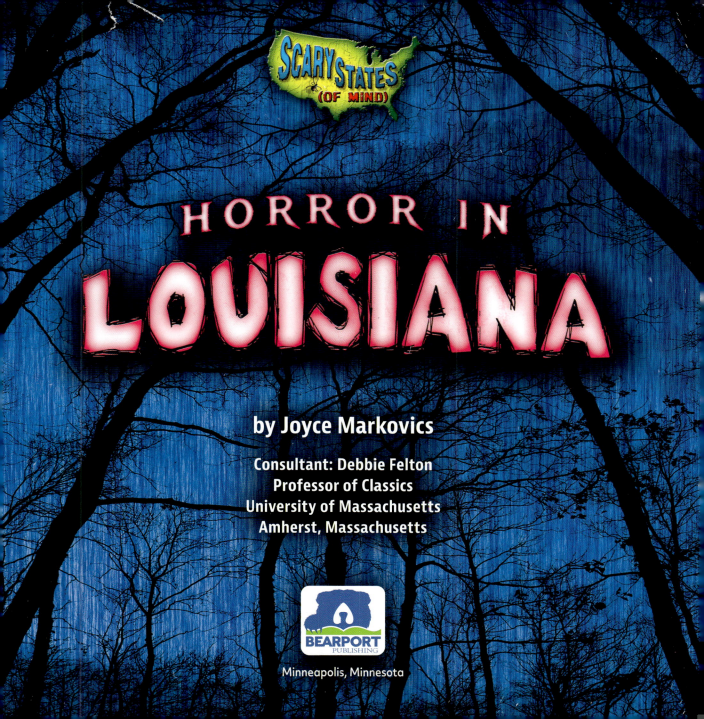

Scary States (of Mind)

HORROR IN LOUISIANA

by Joyce Markovics

Consultant: Debbie Felton
Professor of Classics
University of Massachusetts
Amherst, Massachusetts

BEARPORT PUBLISHING
Minneapolis, Minnesota

Credits

Cover, © Kim Jones, © Runa0410/Shutterstock, © f11photo/Shutterstock, © Jetrel/Shutterstock, © Sergiy1975/Shutterstock, © Kyle T Perry/Shutterstock, and © Roberto Michel/Shutterstock; 3, © Darryl Brooks/Shutterstock; 4-5, © Kim Jones, © Darya Komarova/Shutterstock, and © Chuck Wagner/Shutterstock; 6, © Petinov Sergey Mihilovich/Shutterstock; 7, © Abbie Warnock-Matthews/Shutterstock; 8B, © anyamay/Shutterstock; 9, © f11photo/Shutterstock; 8T, © 3DMI/Shutterstock; 10, Public Domain; 11, © Infrogmation/Wikimedia Commons/Creative Commons; 12, © Everett Collection/Shutterstock; 13, © Jeffrey Isaac Greenberg 4 / Alamy Stock; 14, © tanuha2001/Shutterstock and © rzstudio/Shutterstock; 15, © travelview/Shutterstock; 16, Courtesy Midnight Believer/Find a Grave; 17, © Fer Gregory/Shutterstock; 18, © ranchorunner/Shutterstock; 19, © Cindy Hopkins/Alamy; 20-21, © Ververidis Vasilis/Shutterstock and © duncan1890/iStock; 23, © Havelock Photography/Shutterstock; and 24, © Fer Gregory/Shutterstock.

President: Jen Jenson
Director of Product Development: Spencer Brinker
Editor: Allison Juda
Designer: Micah Edel
Cover: Kim Jones

Library of Congress Cataloging-in-Publication Data

Names: Markovics, Joyce L., author.
Title: Horror in Louisiana / by Joyce Markovics.
Description: Minneapolis, Minnesota : Bearport Publishing Company, 2020. | Series: Scary states (of mind) | Includes bibliographical references and index.
Identifiers: LCCN 2020001864 (print) | LCCN 2020001865 (ebook) | ISBN 9781647470739 (library binding) | ISBN 9781647470838 (ebook)
Subjects: LCSH: Haunted places—Louisiana—Juvenile literature.
Classification: LCC BF1472.U6 M34346 2020 (print) | LCC BF1472.U6 (ebook) | DDC 133.109763—dc23
LC record available at https://lccn.loc.gov/2020001864
LC ebook record available at https://lccn.loc.gov/2020001865

Copyright © 2021 Bearport Publishing Company. All rights reserved. No part of this publication may be reproduced in whole or in part, stored in any retrieval system, or transmitted in any form or by any means, electronic, mechanical, photocopying, recording, or otherwise, without written permission from the publisher.

For more information, write to Bearport Publishing, 5357 Penn Avenue South, Minneapolis, MN 55419. Printed in the United States of America.

CONTENTS

Horror in Louisiana 4
Ghostly Secrets 6
Dining with the Dead 10
A Date with Death 14
Fallen Sailors 18

Spooky Spots in Louisiana................22
Glossary 23
Index 24
Read More 24
Learn More Online 24
About the Author........................24

Horror in Louisiana

Visitors to Louisiana should prepare to be spooked. Almost every old building is said to be haunted. On dark nights, strange voices fill the air. Ghostly figures glide through shadows. Explore the scary side of this southern state.

Get ready to read four spooky stories about Louisiana. Turn the page . . . if you dare.

Ghostly Secrets

Oak Alley Plantation, Vacherie

The branches of twisted, old trees reach like bony fingers across the paths at Oak Alley **Plantation**. But what are they reaching for?

Louise Borne was an office worker at the plantation. She once saw empty rocking chairs begin moving on their own. The chairs rocked back and forth in **unison**. *Creak-creak! Creak-creak!*

Oak Alley Plantation

Oak Alley was once a sugarcane plantation. It used hundreds of enslaved people for labor.

A guide at Oak Alley had an even worse scare. One day during a tour, he saw a candlestick fly across a room! All 35 people on the tour saw the spooky event, too.

Some workers have seen shadowy figures or heard horse hooves on dark nights. Do **spirits** really exist at Oak Alley Plantation?

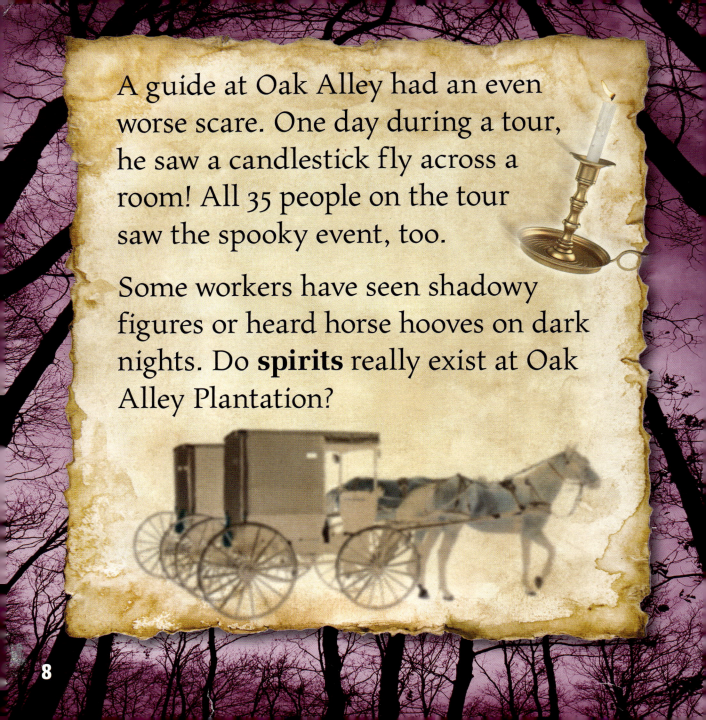

Inside Oak Alley Plantation

Dining with the Dead

Arnaud's, New Orleans

Frenchman Arnaud Cazenave founded Arnaud's restaurant in 1918. People from all over the world visit to try the delicious food . . . and to catch a glimpse of a ghost.

When the dining rooms are busy, waiters often spot a figure in a **tuxedo** that looks like Arnaud. He fixes up the tables. Then, just as quickly as he appears—*poof*—he's gone!

Arnaud Cazenave

Arnaud's restaurant

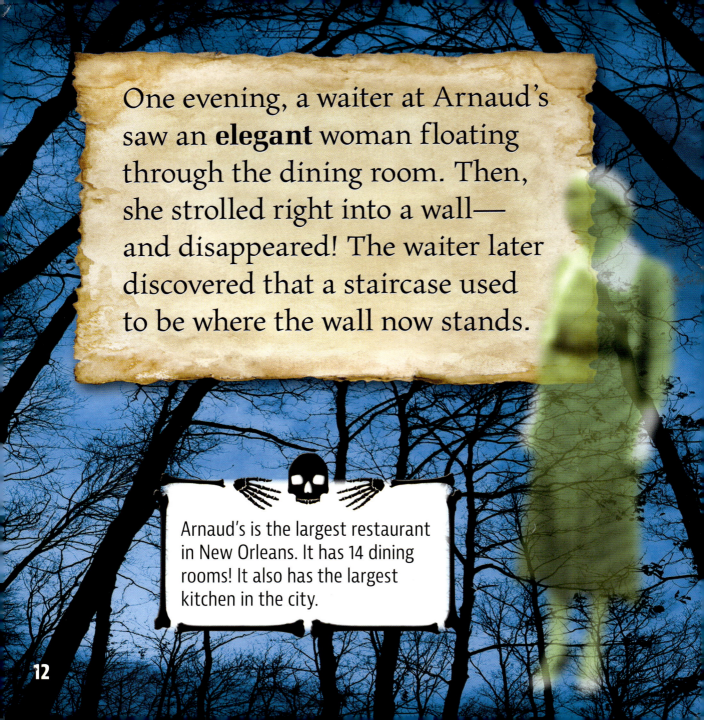

One evening, a waiter at Arnaud's saw an **elegant** woman floating through the dining room. Then, she strolled right into a wall—and disappeared! The waiter later discovered that a staircase used to be where the wall now stands.

Arnaud's is the largest restaurant in New Orleans. It has 14 dining rooms! It also has the largest kitchen in the city.

A dining room at Arnaud's

A Date with Death

Calcasieu Courthouse, Lake Charles

Once inside Calcasieu Courthouse, you might hear a woman screaming. You may smell her perfume, or even worse, her burning hair. Many people believe the spirit of Toni Jo Henry haunts this old courthouse.

Calcasieu Courthouse

Toni Jo decided to break her husband out of prison. But her plan fell apart after she stole a car and killed the car's driver.

After she was caught, Toni Jo was kept in a cell at the Calcasieu Courthouse. She was put to death in the electric chair in 1942. Does her restless spirit remain at the courthouse today?

Toni Jo's hair may have burned when she was **electrocuted**. This might explain why some people smell burning hair in the courthouse.

Toni Jo Henry

Fallen Sailors

USS *Kidd*, Baton Rouge

The USS *Kidd* was a Navy warship during World War II (1939–1945). The ship first launched in 1943 and survived many attacks. However, on April 11, 1945, it wasn't so lucky. A kamikaze (kah-mi-KAH-zee) plane struck the ship. The fiery crash caused a huge explosion, killing 38 sailors and wounding 55 others.

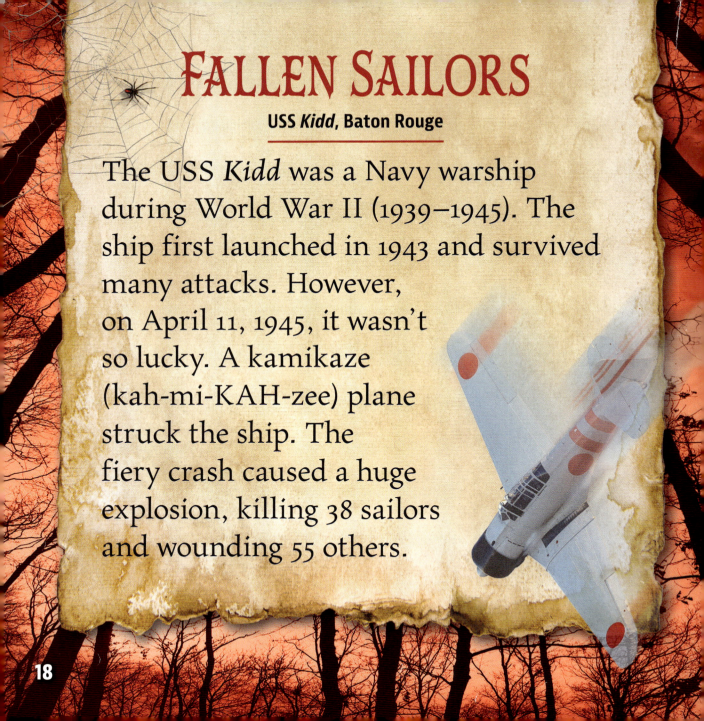

USS *Kidd*

Kamikazes are Japanese planes from World War II. The planes' pilots crashed into ships, giving up their lives to hit enemy targets.

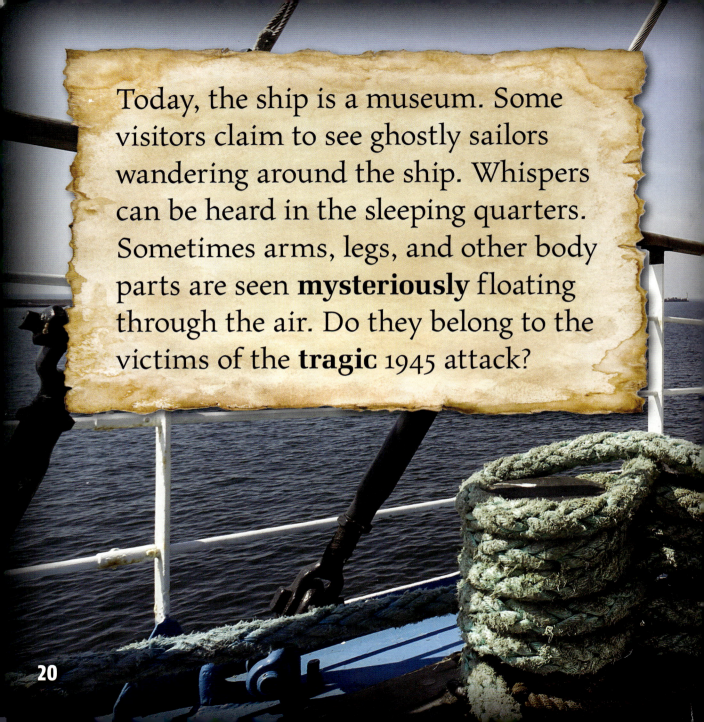

Today, the ship is a museum. Some visitors claim to see ghostly sailors wandering around the ship. Whispers can be heard in the sleeping quarters. Sometimes arms, legs, and other body parts are seen **mysteriously** floating through the air. Do they belong to the victims of the **tragic** 1945 attack?

Spooky Spots in Louisiana

USS KIDD
Visit the spooky sailors at this ship and museum.

OAK ALLEY PLANTATION
Beware the ghostly activity at this southern plantation.

CALCASIEU COURTHOUSE
Watch out for a perfumed killer at this old courthouse.

ARNAUD'S RESTAURANT
Explore a restaurant that serves food and spirits.

GLOSSARY

electrocuted (ih-LEK-truh-kyoot-id) killed by a strong electric shock

elegant (EL-ih-guhnt) having or showing beauty

mysteriously (mih-STEER-ee-uhs-lee) inexplicably or puzzlingly

plantation (plan-TAY-shuhn) a large farm where crops, such as sugarcane or cotton, are grown

spirits (SPIHR-its) ghosts

tragic (TRAJ-ik) very sad or unfortunate

tuxedo (tuhk-SEE-doh) a dark suit often worn with a bow tie

unison (YOO-nuh-suhn) at the same time

INDEX

Arnaud's restaurant 10–12, 22
Baton Rouge 18
Calcasieu Courthouse 14–16, 22
Cazenave, Arnaud 10–11
Henry, Toni Jo 14, 16
kamikazes 18–19
Lake Charles 14
New Orleans 10, 12
Oak Alley Plantation 6–9, 22
sailors 18–20, 22
USS *Kidd* 18–19, 22
Vacherie 6

READ MORE

Merwin, E. *Deserted Cities (Tiptoe Into Scary Places).* New York: Bearport (2018).

Rudolph, Jessica. *Ghost Houses (Tiptoe Into Scary Places).* New York: Bearport (2017).

LEARN MORE ONLINE

1. Go to **www.factsurfer.com**
2. Enter "**Horror in Louisiana**" into the search box.
3. Click on the cover of this book to see a list of websites.

ABOUT THE AUTHOR

Joyce Markovics has written over 100 books for children. She loves old, spooky places and volunteers as a gravestone cleaner in Ossining, New York.